THEY DIED TOO YOUNG

JANIS JOPLIN

Dynise Balcavage

CHELSEA HOUSE PUBLISHERS

The Chelsea House World Wide Web address is
http://www.chelseahouse.com

Printed and bound in The Hashemite Kingdom of Jordan.
First Printing
1 3 5 7 9 8 6 4 2

Cover photo: Janis Joplin (Photofest)

Library of Congress Cataloging-in-Publication Data
Balcavage, Dynise.
    Janis Joplin / Dynise Balcavage.
        p. cm. — (They died too young.)
    Including bibliographical references (p.) and index.
    ISBN 0-7910-5856-5
    1. Joplin, Janis—Juvenile literature. 2. Singers—United States—
Biography—Juvenile literature. [1. Joplin, Janis.   2. Singers.   3. Rock
Music—Biography.   4. Women—Biography.]   I. Title.   II. Series.
ML3930.J65 B35 2000
782.42166'092—dc21
    [B]   00-038395
                                                               CIP

*Our thanks to Michael Joplin for many of the personal photos in
this book. More information on Janis can be found at
www.officialjanis.com.*

Publishing Coordinator Jim McAvoy
Editorial Assistant Rob Quinn
Contributing Editor Amy Handy

ABOUT THE AUTHOR

Dynise Balcavage is the author of *Beethoven, Steroids, The
Great Chicago Fire,* and *The Federal Bureau of Investigation.*
Her work has appeared in numerous magazines, including
Publish, the *Georgia Review,* and *Vital Living.* She lives in
Philadelphia.

CONTENTS

Janis being interviewed in Port Arthur at her 10th
high school reunion.

SEEDS OF REBELLION:
"I THINK I HAVE A VOICE"

Rock star Janis Joplin announced to the world that she would attend her high school reunion at Thomas Jefferson High School in Port Arthur, Texas, during an appearance on *The Dick Cavett Show*. She jokingly asked Cavett if he would like to attend. "Well, Janis, I don't have many friends in your high school class," he said.

"I don't either," she answered, chuckling.

And it was true. Janis's high school days were as bleak as her recent success in music was bright. After enduring years of cruel taunts and loneliness, she was determined to gloat over her musical successes at the reunion.

Once she arrived, reporters peppered Janis with questions about her high school years. Although she had probably dreamed of the perfect answers, she floundered in front of the reporters. The pain was evident in her voice. Even after all those years, the rejection still hurt. But she did manage a few snappy one-liners.

"Did you entertain in high school?" one reporter asked.

"Only when I walked down the aisles," Janis quickly shot back.

The rest of the reunion did not go as Janis would have liked. Her classmates presented her with a tire, a joke gift for having traveled the greatest distance to attend. Despite the fact that she was world famous, that she had recorded successful albums, and that she had seen the world, her classmates remained unimpressed. They rolled their eyes and applauded halfheartedly as she accepted her award. Just as they did during high school, they found Janis's clothes outlandish, and they were confused by her eccentric behavior.

Janis hid her tears behind her dark sunglasses. She still wanted her classmates' approval. But that was never meant to be.

Until the ninth grade, Janis was an ordinary, obedient child, and her life seemed average enough. But things changed during her freshman year of high school. She put on so much weight that her mother took her to a doctor to see if she had a thyroid problem. (The thyroid gland largely regulates people's weight.) But the doctors found nothing remarkable—Janis was simply plump. To make matters worse, she developed a bad case of acne that left her skin pockmarked.

Besides the normal physical transformations of puberty, something in Janis's personality also clicked, and she began to express her opinions. At that time, for example, blacks and whites were still largely segregated, but the foundation of integration—sending all children regardless of race to the same schools—was taking root. During a conversation about integration, Janis mentioned that she thought the idea was "fine." She suffered when two of her schoolmates taunted her about it.

Janis seemed to take comfort in people whose differences had also caused them pain. Two of her closest friends in high school, Karleen and Arlene Elster, were Jewish, while the overwhelming majority of families in the area were either Catholic or Baptist. She also grew very close to an African-American woman who worked as a housekeeper for the Joplins.

With her rough manner, love of jokes, and lack of concern for her appearance, Janis was considered more like one of the guys than a "girly girl." Around 10th grade she started hanging out with boys others considered bad company. It seemed natural for Janis to go against the tide—to hang around with outcasts, to be unconcerned with projecting the ideal feminine image of the time, to say what she wanted to say without regard for what others thought of her. At a time when most·so-called "good girls" wore bobby socks, loafers, crisp white shirts, and modest skirts, Janis found clothes to be tools for self-expression. Her skirts, for example, were cut above the knee, when the other girls' skirts fell below the calf.

"Was it loud enough? . . . Was it irritating enough?" Janis would ask her childhood friend Karleen Bennett about her antics. But besides Bennett and a few other friends, most of Janis's classmates did not accept her outspoken individuality. Janis was often the target of their practical jokes and ruthless teasing.

"Janis would laugh . . . playing along to get along," Bennett remembers. "But she'd go home and cry."

Yet not everyone tormented Janis. Adrian Haston, Randy Tenant, Jim Langdon, Dave Moriaty, and Grant Lyons became her best friends. The six teens had a lot in common. They were all adventurous, and they were all intelligent. And many people in Port Arthur felt they were all a bit odd. They devoured books; they even read more than their teachers assigned. They were enamored of jazz music. With Texas being so flat the six teenagers also often climbed the highest vantage points, to look out beyond the clipped Port Arthur skyline. The gang often drove across the state line to Vinton, Louisiana, where they went to bars and listened to white soul bands like the Boogie Kings and Jerry LaCroix and the Counts.

Initially, the five boys did not like the idea of Janis hanging around. Certainly she was not like the other high school girls; neither pretty nor sweet, she was not exactly what they considered girlfriend material. But her wild side helped change their minds. In fact, Janis was probably a bit wilder than the boys.

"Everybody began to realize she was fun to have around because she raised so much hell," remembered Dave Moriaty. "By the time we were in mid-high school, she was one of our favorite characters. I hate to think of how we treated her sometimes. She occupied about the position of court jester!"

Thanks to magazines like *Time,* Janis learned about a disenchanted group of young people called the beatniks—people who questioned authority and social conventions and instead indulged in self-expression. Awestruck and inspired, she read about this alternative to the stifling conformity that fenced her in. Although Janis did not know it at the time, she and her five friends were more or less Port Arthur's own set of beats.

Janis's parents did not encourage her openness to diversity or her unorthodox tastes. Her parents listened to Mozart, but much to their chagrin, Janis was naturally drawn to the blues, folk music and jazz. Even though most young people during this time embraced rock and roll, Janis despised it. "It seemed so shallow, all oop-boop," she later recalled. She preferred more unusual expression. She was entranced by the soulful sounds of Huddie "Leadbelly" Ledbetter. His music, she said, was "like a flash. It *mattered* to me."

The first singer Janis tried to imitate was Odetta. An African American born in Los Angeles, Odetta became the era's quintessential folk singer. Janis practiced singing to her records. One day among her friends, Janis burst into an Odetta song, sounding exactly like her.

She "showed us up," Moriaty recalls. "We used to sing folk songs on our way driving anywhere. Well, after that, we still did, but it wasn't the same. We weren't all in the same class anymore." Her friends were silenced by her soulful outburst.

"Hey, I think I have a voice," Janis announced.

Her parents seemed strict, but in some ways they were permissive. Her father tolerated her antics much more than her mother did. When Mr. Joplin had to deal with Janis's attention-grabbing hijinks, he tried to appeal to her intellect by reasoning with her. On the other hand, Mrs. Joplin argued on the basis of fitting in and of doing what everyone else was doing. She begged her daughter to "be like everybody else," which, of course, only inspired her to rebel more.

When she wasn't hanging out with the gang, Janis spent a great deal of time painting, especially canvases of nudes. Her parents tried to redirect their daughter's artistic energies toward landscapes, a more socially acceptable form of expression. Mr. Joplin even drove Janis to Pleasure Pier in an attempt to inspire her to paint seascapes. According to Karleen Bennett, Janis once painted a nude on her closet door; when Mrs. Joplin disapproved, Janis had to "clothe" the naked figure with drawings of fish.

At the request of her mother, in Janis's senior year she focused her artistic talent in a drafting class. Her peers teased her unmercifully because she was the only girl in the class. She also joined several other clubs that her mother approved of—the Future Nurses of America, the Future Teachers of America, and the art club.

Always looking beyond the horizon, Janis wanted to take a trip to New Orleans, the famous honky-tonk city of music, nightlife, and liquor. Knowing the city's reputation, Janis's parents denied her permission to visit the town with her friends. But that did not stop her.

Janis told her parents she needed to borrow the car and that she was sleeping over her friend Karleen's house. Instead, she picked up three of her male pals, including Jim Langdon, and made her way to New Orleans. Her original plan was to get back before morning so her parents would be none the wiser.

The four teens spent the night exploring the edgy city with its jazz joints and numerous bars. On the way home after a wild night, Janis was too sleepy to drive, so her friend Clyde took the wheel. Famous for his hot-rod driving, Clyde got into a minor accident. The police stopped the group and phoned Janis's parents. According to Janis's sister Laura, her older sister's behavior "was so bad, our parents didn't know what to say about it."

The Joplins were relieved when their daughter enrolled in Lamar State College of Technology in nearby Beaumont. Given the difficulties she endured in high school, they did not even think she would go to college. But still, they hoped her rebellion was just a phase.

It soon became evident there was no holding Janis back.

Janis's first day of school in 1955.

GROWING UP IN PORT ARTHUR

Seth Joplin, Janis's father, dropped out of Texas A&M University's engineering program with only one semester to go. He left Amarillo and headed to Port Arthur, where he got a job pumping gas. A docile man who kept to himself, he often said he would have made a good monk; he lived simply and delved into books whenever he had the chance. A few years later, a friend recommended him for a job as an engineer for Texaco.

Dorothy Joplin's family moved to Amarillo from Nebraska when she was a high school senior. An intelligent, hard-working woman, Dorothy was known for her strong opinions. Her beautiful voice earned her a college scholarship to Texas Christian University. But she did not enjoy college and returned to Amarillo.

At a time when most women did not work, Dorothy ignored conventions and built her career. She started with a temporary job at the Montgomery Ward department store and did so well that she was soon promoted to department head. She later worked as a registrar at an area college. When she was 22, she moved to Port Arthur, where she met Seth on a blind date. In 1936, the couple married after dating for a year.

The newlyweds moved to a house surrounded at the time by a cushion of undeveloped land and overlooking an open field. Their first child, Janis Lyn Joplin, arrived on January 19, 1943, at St. Mary's Hospital.

Janis was a slight infant, weighing in at only 5 pounds, 8 ounces, but she grew quickly and was relatively carefree. Her independent nature showed itself at an early age: she ate with a fork and spoon and drank from a cup instead of a bottle at only 11 months of age. Janis's childhood pictures portray a happy toddler, curious and full of life.

Like her father, she became an avid reader. Janis was fascinated by books and applied for a library card as as soon as she was old enough. She often escaped into the worlds between the pages.

An extremely artistic child, Janis began to draw as soon as she could hold a pencil. Mrs. Joplin recognized her talent and treated her to private art lessons when she was in third and fourth grade.

Young Janis did not exhibit any exceptional musical talents or interests. Around the time of her sixth birthday, Mrs. Joplin bought her a piano and showed her how to play some children's tunes. But a thyroid operation had severed Mrs. Joplin's vocal chords and left her unable to sing. Soon, listening to her young daughter playing and singing proved to be too painful for the woman whose angelic voice had once earned her a college scholarship. Mr. Joplin sold the piano.

Janis sang herself to sleep as a child and was a member of the church choir and glee club in junior high school. Fascinated by myths and fables, she invented countless stories. She loved to study tall tales of America, and she amused her family and friends with her magical, invented accounts.

When Janis was six, her sister Laura was born. Not long after, the Joplins moved to a better neighborhood in Port Arthur. Unlike Janis, Laura was a sickly baby and needed a lot of attention and care. Laura's constant demands exhausted Mrs. Joplin and left her with even less time to spend with Janis.

But, according to her mother, Janis heartily accepted her baby sibling and did not feel the least bit jealous. In fact, she enjoyed her role as the protective big sister and spent a great deal of time looking after Laura. "She watched her with more concern than I did," Mrs. Joplin confessed.

Around this time, Janis began writing plays and performing them with her friends. Mr. Joplin built Janis a wonderful puppet theater that she and her pals used as a stage for their shows. Since she had the theater, a sandbox, trees, and animals, Janis's backyard became a gathering place for neighborhood children, and Janis often directed the group's activities.

An excellent student, Janis was accelerated to the third grade. When she was 10, her brother Michael arrived, and just as she did with Laura, Janis happily accepted her newest sibling.

By this point, though, Janis did demand more attention from her parents, possibly because of the arrival of her two younger siblings. A competitive child, she was determined to be taller than her classmates, to earn better grades, and to win at activities. She needed to excel. And she

Janis with her newborn brother Michael Ross, 1953.

also demonstrated a stubborn streak. One night, for instance, she sat at the dinner table until bedtime rather than finishing her turnips. Usually, though, Janis was a serene child, lost in the vivid world of her own imagination. Her parents rarely needed to discipline her.

The Joplins encouraged Janis to read and urged her to think beyond the boundaries of the books. Mrs. Joplin felt all her children should develop minds of their own and discuss their ideas. "We included the children in all our conversations, and we wanted them to voice their opinions and ideas about everything," she said.

She was also taught that there was more to life than Port Arthur. Her father often took her to the post office, where they read the FBI's Most Wanted posters. Janet learned that the world wasn't always a safe place, and that not everyone was to be trusted. But she also learned that there was room in the world for people who were different.

**Janis, second from left, at a Thomas Jefferson High School pep
rally during her junior year.**

Despite living in such a small town, Janis developed an
interest in all kinds of music. Through radio she grew up
hearing country, jazz, blues, Cajun, gospel, Mexican and
Caribbean rhythms, along with classical, folk and pop music.
Unfortunately, the Port Arthur community labeled different
forms of music as good, bad, or even "devil's music." Janis
learned not to show an interest in the so-called wrong type
of music, but she continued to enjoy all kinds of music.

They Died Too Young

Extremely cooperative and a bit shy, Janis also continued to excel in elementary school. An excellent, industrious student, Janis earned good grades. She volunteered at the library and at her church. She won an art contest and created posters for the library. She belonged to the bridge club.

She certainly enjoyed a wonderful childhood. But those days were not to last. Soon, her own free will and the opinions that her parents encouraged her to form came to the surface. As she got ready to enter high school, she could not help but say what she thought and honestly express the ideas—no matter how different from the norm—that took root in her mind.

"Then the whole world turned!" she explained. "It just turned on me."

58-59

THOMAS JEFFERSON HI.

Janis, seen here in a high school photo, never really felt accepted as a teen.

A studio portrait, 1960.

ESCAPE FROM THE GREAT NOWHERE

Life at Lamar College was infinitely better than life in Port Arthur. For one thing, Janis was no longer such an outcast. Several of her best high school friends—Jim Langdon, Adrian Haston, and Tary Owens—were also enrolled there, and Lamar collected rebels from all over east Texas. But even here, people began to break off into groups, and the "good" girls spread rumors that Janis was promiscuous.

Classes bored Janis, probably because she was so intelligent. With no one to monitor her life, Janis often skipped school. Still, she could not bear to be second best at anything. She actually gave up painting after another student, Tommy Stopher, turned out to be a better artist than she was. At least when she was being outrageous, no one else came close to outdoing her.

Janis loved to spend long hours in the Beaumont bars with her friends, drinking beer and talking. They had soul-searching discussions about cultural topics. They read the most talked-about books of the time—including Lawrence Ferlinghetti's *A Coney Island of the Mind* and Jean-Paul Sartre's *No Exit*—and they often stayed up all night analyzing and interpreting them. They played music and listened to records.

For a time, Janis and her new friends Dave McQueen and Patti Skaff were inseparable. "We were constantly together, and we related to each other very intensely," McQueen remembers. "We felt like outlaws and renegades in that culture and we were trying very hard to be hip."

Campus life at Lamar seemed dull to Janis. School officials kept a tight watch on female students. They even expelled a 24-year-old divorcée for walking on the dormitory terrace in a bikini. Janis and her friends responded to the rules by sneaking out after curfew check to attend off-campus drinking parties.

Janis had fun with her friends, but she detested the academics, so at the end of the fall term she moved back in with her parents and took a few secretarial courses at Port Arthur College. She began cutting classes again, but since her parents would not allow her to move out of Port Arthur unless she got her secretarial certificate, she grudgingly put in enough time. In 1961 she earned her certificate and headed to Los Angeles, the birthplace of Odetta, her childhood idol.

Mrs. Joplin had two sisters in Los Angeles and felt they could help her retain some control over her rebellious daughter. Yet Janis's time there was like a game of "musical apartments." She moved in with her Aunt Mimi and got a job as a keypunch operator, which, not surprisingly, she despised. She moved in with her Aunt Barbara; then, anxious to get out on her own, Janis leased a place in a rather seedy neighborhood of Venice, California.

Although the spartan flat left much to be desired, Janis liked the area's coffeehouses and its edginess. She sang at the Gas House a few times, but when Venice's touristy facade began to crumble, she left town and hitchhiked to North Beach. After a few months, she surprised everyone by returning to Port Arthur unannounced.

Like many people her age, Janis went through a period of indecisiveness about her life's direction. After some soul-searching, she decided to reenroll at Lamar. Pleased with this decision, her parents were a bit easier on her. They said she could do what she wanted as long as she attended church and kept up with her schoolwork. When her father offered to front half the money for a car, Janis took a waitressing job to earn the rest.

Things seemed different for a bit, but soon the familiar patterns began to reappear. Trips to bars across the state line resumed, as did Janis's rebellious behavior. One day Janis and her friends drove to Austin and were greeted by a folk-singer named John Clay, who was perched atop a refrigerator plucking on a banjo, with a bottle of wine wedged between his knees. Janis smiled at her friends. "I'm gonna' love it here." She quit Lamar once again and enrolled at the University of Texas at Austin in the summer of 1962. She also rented an apartment.

In Austin, instead of being harassed for her individuality, Janis was praised for it. The campus newspaper even wrote an article about her entitled "She Dares to Be Different"—quite a contrast from the way she was treated in Port Arthur.

And Janis *was* different, especially compared to the bouffant hairdos and modest skirts of the other girls. Janis went barefoot, wore jeans to class, and carried her Autoharp at all times, just in case she got inspired to burst into song, which she often did. It was here that Janis had her first encounter with drugs. She and her friends tried marijuana and amphetamines (speed). She even experimented with the hallucinogenic drug LSD.

Janis also began to experiment more seriously with music. Every Wednesday night, she and a group of friends would meet in the student union, taking turns singing and playing instruments. When Janis's turn came, people had no choice but to listen to her powerful voice. Her raw talent was obvious, as was her ability to convey complex emotions through her voice. The group applauded wildly whenever she finished a song.

Janis became obsessed with music, studying and listening to all types, practicing almost every night. When a friend recognized her talent and suggested that she take voice lessons, Janis refused. "They'd only want me to sing differently," she contended. She was probably right.

Janis and her friends showcased their talents on Wednesday evenings at Threadgill's, an old gas station converted into a bar by its owner, Kenneth Threadgill, an accomplished yodeler. Over time the audience grew from a handful of locals to a packed house, thanks to Janis's voice.

Janis's musical idol, Odetta, on her self-titled album.

At that time she had not yet refined her own style, and resorted mostly to imitating singers she admired: Joan Baez and Judy Collins, and her heroine, Odetta. Performing at Threadgill's, Janis was in her glory; she could not quite believe that all those people were coming to hear her sing. But the thunderous applause said it all.

Her elation did not last for long. In October 1962 the fraternities at the University of Texas at Austin held an annual contest—the ugliest man on campus. Male contestants representing the various fraternities tried to drum up votes by walking around the university in outrageous outfits. Contestants' names were listed on a campus message board. One friend, Powell St. John, remembers seeing Janis weep after discovering her name on the board. Janis did not win the contest but just being listed was bad enough.

The butt of another cruel joke, Janis realized she could not live her life the way she wanted to in Texas. When Chet Helms, a friend and former engineering student who sometimes played in her band, suggested that they hitchhike to San Francisco, Janis packed her bags and did not look back.

Janis's first publicity shot, photographed by a friend in
Austin, Texas, 1963.

THE BUTTERFLY

Within about 50 hours, Janis and Chet made their way to San Francisco in January 1963. There she found a world of art, music, literature, and poetry. She knew that she could finally live the "beat" life she craved.

She made it clear that she was coming to San Francisco to sing, and thanks to Chet she got a gig her very first night. Apparently, Janis's performance so moved the audience that they actually passed around a hat to collect money for her, something that had never been done in the coffeehouse. Later, she performed a few blocks down at another coffeehouse, the Coffee Gallery.

Even though he had no real experience, Chet turned out to be an excellent manager. He arranged for Janis to perform at several coffeehouses in a neighborhood called South Bay, where she met other soon-to-be-famous musicians, including Jorma Kaukonen, who later played guitar with the group Jefferson Airplane.

At the Coffee Gallery, Janis met Linda Gottfreid, who had been in the city for only a day and had nowhere to stay. Janis invited her to stay in her apartment, a basement on Sacramento Street where she was living rent-free, thanks to the generosity of some fellow folksingers. Janis and Linda became fast friends. They both had tense relationships with their families and were both lonely.

Even though she did not have to pay rent, Janis barely scraped by on the meager pay she earned singing. She received an unemployment check and also took to shoplifting, a habit that got her arrested during her second month in town.

In San Francisco, drugs were widely available, and many of the beats considered getting high an essential part of the creative process. In their eyes, it allowed them easier access to the part of their subconscious that ruled free expression.

23

And since almost all the beat celebrities—including poet Allen Ginsberg, writers William Burroughs and Jack Kerouac, and most of the era's musicians—experimented with drugs, young people strived to emulate them. Using speed, liquor, and marijuana was just part of an ordinary day.

When they first encountered the abundance of available drugs, Janis and Linda were thrilled by their effect. "We thought we were growing by leaps and bounds," Linda said. "We worked night and day. We did more paintings, more poems, and more songs."

But Janis was disciplined about her music. She spent a good part of the day analyzing songs and practicing. "She studied Leadbelly, Billie Holiday, Bessie Smith," said Linda. "On Sundays, we'd go to various black churches and sit in the back and do gospel. . . . I mean, she *worked*."

Once again, Janis was gaining a reputation—but this time it was based on her voice, not her appearance. She performed at many local bars and coffeehouses. "It got to the point that no other female singers wanted to perform when she showed up at hootenannies [singalongs]," recalled Linda. Wherever she sang, her voice held the audience spellbound.

When it came to the blues, Janis was a purist. She lived for the raw, unmapped electric dirges that were becoming a foundation of the city's music scene. She felt she had no right to sing the blues unless she lived them, too. Amazingly, in spite of all the pain she had already endured, Janis felt she had not suffered enough to convey a true sense of loneliness and longing in her music. "A lot of artists have one way of art and another of life," Janis explained. "They're the same for me."

Janis spent much of her young adulthood trying to laugh off all the insults. But in San Francisco, drugs and alcohol seemed to break down the floodgates that held back her feelings. Any emotion she had demonstrated through her singing back in Texas had only scratched the surface of how she really felt. When she did drugs, Janis actually experienced the pain. As a result, her music became edgier, more

They Died Too Young

tormented. The only problem was that so did Janis, and she was not equipped to confront these latent emotions.

Janis's voice began to stand out from other popular female folksingers of the time. While the public adored the pretty sounds of Joan Baez, Judy Collins, and Buffy Ste. Marie, they did not readily accept Janis's brutal, sometimes dissonant voice. Often onstage, she would launch into a 10-minute scream session—anchored with raw pain and anger. Although many San Francisco music critics appreciated Janis's style and knew she was onto something unique, most people neither accepted nor understood her music. In fact, back in Texas, she was once kicked offstage during one of her impassioned vocal outbursts. But she would not compromise her budding vocal style—or her funky way of dressing. She showed up at gigs with frizzy, uncombed hair, wearing tattered blue jeans and a crumpled man's shirt.

Likewise, she did not make many compromises during her daily life. Perhaps because she had been through enough tauntings back in Texas, Janis had no patience for propriety in San Francisco. If she was in a conversation with someone who was boring her, she would simply cut them off midsentence. Once, as she was leaving a bar called the Anxious Asp, a group of bikers stared at her. Janis did not like their gawking, so she yelled at them. They ganged up on her and beat her badly. In some ways, life in San Francisco was easier, but in other ways, Janis endured as much of a struggle as in Texas.

Once again, Janis looked beyond the horizon, hoping that another city would save her. Life in San Francisco was so concentrated that she needed to escape for a while. This time she headed east to New York City, thinking she might make it there as a singer. She wasted no time in finding a place to live. She shared an apartment on the Lower East Side with Janice and Ed Knoll. She and Janice became friends and often took speed together. They talked about their families, philosophy, and music.

Suprisingly, Janis's mother sent her some glitzy outfits, including an embroidered blouse encrusted with tiny mirrors and a long, plush tapestry robe. She adamantly refused to wear them, because she felt they were too flashy.

Soon Janis was singing the blues at Slug's, a club in Manhattan's East Village. Whenever she sang there, she always wore the same attire—black jeans and a black V-neck sweater with a huge gold watch hanging from a necklace. Strangely enough, people in New York did not find her at all unusual. But Janis was used to standing out. By fall 1964, after only four months in New York City, she had had enough of the Big Apple. Once again, Janis hit the road and made her way back to San Francisco. On the way back, she made an unannounced visit to Port Arthur. She gave her sister, who was then 15, an old, battered guitar. Although it was warped and practically unplayable, Laura was moved by the gesture.

Janis never seemed to have trouble finding a place to stay, but then again, she did not seem to care much about the conditions in which she lived. This time she took shelter in a small, filthy boardinghouse on Geary Street.

She brought her speed habit back with her, and by the end of the year, she was undeniably addicted, as were her friends Chet and Linda. She began selling drugs to make extra cash. She and her friends were constantly strung out on speed. One day when she had no speed, Janis tried to shoot up watermelon juice. She knew she had a drug problem but did not know how to stop.

In May 1965, alone and scared, Janis tried to check herself into San Francisco General, a mental hospital. Ironically, they turned her away, since many people at the time tried to fake mental illness in order to gain a place to stay. But Janis truly thought she was losing her mind.

If her addiction was not trouble enough, Janis was also having trouble finding a serious, caring relationship. She dated both men and women but could not really relate to anyone on a genuine level. The longest any relationship

They Died Too Young

would last was a few weeks. Janis felt lonely and unfulfilled, and the emptiness may have fueled her speed habit.

The one man with whom she became somewhat seriously involved was Michel Raymond (not his real name). His past was colorful and mysterious enough to attract Janis, and they shot speed together. He was a genius with electronics and claimed to have a graduate degree from McGill University. He also claimed to have served in the French army in Algeria, and he told friends that he worked for the FBI. Many of Janis's friends thought he was severely unstable. The fact was that Michel grew up in Niagara Falls, New York, and according to some friends, never even attended college. He got an East Coast girlfriend pregnant, married her, and then left her after only a few months. Janis's friends were concerned over her new relationship. But Janis adored him, probably because she could be herself when she was with him.

Janis was literally starving. At one point, friends became concerned because she was not eating. The once-chunky girl was now so thin that friends actually brought her food from the grocery store and begged her to eat. Speed was her only nourishment, but it was killing her—and Janis knew it. After suffering from speed paranoia, Janis's boyfriend ended up at San Francisco General for almost two weeks.

Even though she reveled in the fast San Francisco lifestyle, a part of Janis still craved acceptance and normalcy. Frightened by her own addiction and by her boyfriend's, she resolved to clean up her act, move back to Port Arthur, and marry Michel. In May 1965, a few of Janis's friends threw her a going away party, at which they all pitched in money for her busfare home.

Once again, Janis decided to give Lamar another try. She enrolled earnestly as a sociology major. This time, determined to be a good student, she decided to abstain from drugs, alcohol, and even singing. Even though the weather was hot and sticky in Texas, Janis wore long-sleeved dresses to hide the needle tracks that were still healing on her arms. She told her parents she was going to get married to Michel, who remained back in San Francisco.

Janis began counseling with Bernard Giarratano, a social worker. She found she could confide in him, so she told him about how depressed she had been feeling and how her experimentation with drugs had frightened her enough to try to change. She confessed that she wanted to be more like her younger sister, Laura, who seemed the epitome of what a young Texas lady should be—proper, well-spoken, pretty, and studious.

All of Janis's differences caused her problems in an unaccepting world. Even her superior mind caused her grief. She often challenged things her professors had taught and, unsure how to handle her questions, they rebuked her. Still, in the winter of 1965, she earned above-average grades. But she was not happy, because she was focusing her energy and emotion on becoming some woman that she was never meant to be. She was, in a sense, acting.

When her old pal Jim Langdon tried to persuade her to sing again, she refused, though she still listened to the blues. In November, Mrs. Joplin asked her daughter to paint a nativity scene for the front porch. Janis obediently complied. Her mother began sewing a wedding gown for her, and Janis started piecing together a Lone Star quilt for her hope chest. Michel even called Mr. Joplin to formally request his daughter's hand in marriage. But no wedding would take place—it was just another elaborate fantasy; he had no intention of marrying Janis. This rejection shattered Janis. It seemed to solidify the fact that she could not conform to the traditional life she craved, no matter how hard she tried.

Janis found solace in music. She began singing again, but tried to tone down her act a bit, showing up for gigs with her hair coiled up in a bun, wearing a black suit and heels. But the voice did not match the look..Although she could disguise herself with clothes, her powerful voice could not be contained. She continued to perform at Austin's Eleventh Door, to mostly welcoming crowds who fed her hunger for acceptance with wild applause. She did not have to try to sing; it just came naturally, and it felt good when an audience appreciated her voice, because she spent so much of her energy searching for reinforcement.

Janis was going to join an Austin band called the 13th Floor Elevators when a San Francisco friend named Travis Rivers came to visit. Chet sent him on a mission to persuade Janis to return to San Francisco to join a band called Big Brother and the Holding Company. Janis loved the idea, but she was terrified of the drugs—of not being able to say no to them.

She called Chet and asked him to promise he would buy her a bus ticket home if she did not want to stay. Reassured but a bit uneasy, on May 30 she once again left Texas with Travis and a few friends. They arrived in San Francisco on June 5.

San Francisco had changed its clothes. If it was colorful before, now it was downright kaleidoscopic. Artists and beats from all over the country and the world flocked there, drawn to its bohemian pulse. Anyone who was doing anything in the arts knew San Francisco was the place to be.

Janis auditioned for Big Brother, and the other members—Dave Getz, James Gurley, Sam Andrews, and Peter Albin—voted unanimously to let her join.

In 1966, rock and roll was still in its early years, and Janis was used to singing the blues and folk. Learning to sing over the sound of an electric guitar, bass, and drums was a real challenge, but they practiced in an old barn and eventually Janis was able to overpower even the loudest equipment. Once, the police banged on the door when they were rehearsing. They had gotten a report of a woman screaming and they came by to investigate. It was only Janis singing.

Besides possessing a gutsy, acid voice, Janis had a real stage presence. She pranced and strutted around the stage, alternating between screaming at the top of her lungs and

Janis Joplin with Big Brother and the Holding Company.

whispering so quietly she could hardly be heard. Audiences were mesmerized.

Janis tried to improve her looks. A dermatologist treated her acne. Back in Texas, dressing down was a form of self-expression, but in Haight-Ashbury, outrageous clothes were all the rage. In thrift stores, Janis bought a selection of items the hippies were wearing at the time—a poncho and a madras dress. She loaded dozens of bracelets on her wrists and wrapped feather boas around her neck. She also became a student of soul music and listened to her new heroes, Tina Turner and Otis Redding. The band played just about every weekend and spent almost all of their time together; they even shared a house. In the midst of all this change, Janis was struggling to keep away from drugs, but the temptation was always in the air. Drugs were even more common than when she first lived in San Francisco.

Most of Janis's friends had paired up, but she did not have a steady lover, although she did have a few boyfriends.

They Died Too Young

Her old friend Chet Helms decided to stop managing Big Brother. She was lonely, and her defenses were down. Since her circle of friends and the other members of Big Brother were all shooting speed, Janis eventually succumbed to the temptation. She also experimented with heroin but only a few times. If she was going to do speed recreationally, at least she was determined to stay clean of harder drugs.

Around this time, Janis became friends with Linda Gravenites, a fashion designer. The two talked about everything and grew very close. Linda ended up designing many of Janis's clothes and offering her advice on her career.

Over a three-day period in June 1967, more than 30 bands gathered to entertain a captive audience of mostly hippies and beats at the County Fairgrounds at Monterey. Unlike the world-renowned band the Who and electric guitar virtuoso Jimi Hendrix, Big Brother was one of the festival's lesser-known acts.

But not for long. Janis slithered out in a satiny silver-white pants suit. She tapped her foot, writhed to the music, shared her pain, joy, and sadness, and the audience was smitten. They watched her every move onstage and waited to see what antics she would pull next. The girl from Texas had transformed herself into a shimmering butterfly, emitting all the colors that were never visible beneath her thick cocoon.

As luck would have it, representatives from just about every major record label in the country were in attendance, as well as many other musical professionals.

Janis and Big Brother and the Holding Company attend the press party celebrating their signing with CBS Records. Manager Albert Grossman is seen at left, and Clive Davis, president of Columbia Records, is on Janis's left.

FALLING

Newsweek and *Time* gave Big Brother's Monterey performance rave reviews. Not surprisingly, Clive Davis, then president of Columbia Records, was interested in offering them a record contract.

They later hooked up with Albert Grossman, a well-seasoned rock manager who helped Big Brother negotiate their contract with Columbia. At the bargaining table, he warned the band about heroin. "There's one thing I won't have anything to do with and that's smack. I've seen terrible things with it and if anybody here is messing with it at all, there's no point in going any further," he stated. "We can call it quits before we start!" The entire group nodded soberly in agreement.

Janis spent her days rehearsing and her evenings and weekends performing. She lost weight and gained confidence. She carried herself with more dignity. All these positive feelings filtered into her voice, and onstage she was even more mesmerizing than before.

Bob Shelton, a rock critic from the *New York Times,* heard Big Brother play and gave them more rave reviews. He printed a photo of Janis, which snowballed into a great deal more media exposure for the band. In a matter of months, the group went from San Francisco coffeehouse band to famous musicians. *Crawdaddy* and *Rolling Stone* also touted the band's talents, particularly Janis's soulful voice.

She loved all the attention, but at the same time, it terrified her—swinging from one extreme of rejection to the other of adulation. The band began touring, first in New York, then in Boston, Cleveland, and Detroit. Unfortunately, they played terribly; their instruments were out of tune, and their timing was off.

Janis, on the other hand, glowed. Onstage she was transformed into a frenzy of screams, twinkling jewelry, gyrating hips, and playful antics. The audiences loved it. They stood up clapping, screaming, and begging for more. They didn't seem to notice the less-than-polished band behind her.

Janis and Linda rented an apartment together, and around the same time, Big Brother began recording their first album under the Columbia contract. According to Elliot Mazer, who helped edit the album, unlike the other members of Big Brother, Janis was almost obsessed with the album's quality. "For two weeks, only Janis, myself, and the engineer would stay, from two in the afternoon until seven in the morning. . . . I never *knew* an artist that worked harder. She was twenty times more serious than any of those people in that band!"

The album, called *Cheap Thrills,* featured an R. Crumb cartoon on the cover. Even though everything in her life looked rosy, Janis was often depressed and let her nasty temper display itself over and over during this period. She became short and sarcastic, and she had little patience for anyone.

Maybe to soothe her depression, Janis began drinking heavily. As a result, she gained back the weight she had lost. Emotionally, she was on a downward spiral.

Yet from the outside, her world seemed idyllic. Janis acquired a great deal of money from her performances, and she handled her money wisely. She did allow herself some luxuries, though. She bought herself a Porsche, a nice home, and extravagant clothes. She also bought lots of drugs.

The promoters changed the name of the band on the concert billing to "Janis Joplin with Big Brother and the Holding Company." This caused a certain amount of friction with the other band members. They didn't like all the attention Janis was getting. In their minds, they were around first: they had made Janis.

Cheap Thrills was released in August 1968. The band decided to break up not much later, but they finished up their fall shows. The morning before their last performance, Janis

**Janis and Big Brother bathed in the psychedelic colors
of the Joshua Light Show at the Fillmore East, 1968.**

had trouble sleeping. A friend gave her some Seconal (a sleeping pill), which she washed down with Southern Comfort (a hard liquor). Before the concert, she downed speed.

Besides smoking pot and drinking, Janis began experimenting with exactly the drug that Grossman had warned her against. Given her state of loneliness and depression, combined with the tremendous peer pressure, it was difficult to resist. According to Janis, heroin kept her from "feeling bad."

At the apartment on Noe Street, Janis shot up, but this time was different. Her drug abuse caught up to her, and she overdosed. She survived only because Linda and another friend, Pat "Sunshine" Nichols, revived her with a salt solution and ice water. They slapped her until her body sported polka-dot welts, but they kept her awake and alive.

Janis started rehearsals for her solo tour in 1969 and formed her own band. They had only a few weeks to practice before they went out on tour in the United States and Europe. Their first concerts in 1969 in the Midwest and on the East Coast were mediocre at best, but their performances in Amsterdam, Copenhagen, Stockholm, Paris, and London went well. The European audiences loved the band.

They began recording an album, *I Got Dem Ol' Kozmic Blues Again Mama*. The sessions went badly because everyone was on edge. They all blamed each other for how badly the recording was going. Janis steered clear of pot during the recording, but at night she downed liquor to soothe her pain. She was struggling to stay clean, but once again she succumbed to heroin's powerful appeal. In spite of her using, she did not miss a performance. Often she took several drugs simultaneously to numb the tremendous hurt and loneliness she was feeling.

Drug users often indulge so they do not have to deal with powerful emotional issues such as the ones that were coming up in Janis's life—of not being pretty enough or "proper" enough, of not being worthy to live and to enjoy life. These messages were ingrained in Janis since her school days. So she deadened the pain the only way she knew. As self-destructive as it seems, in Janis's eyes it was a survival tactic. "Maybe my audiences can enjoy my music more if they think I'm destroying myself," she quipped.

Janis began seeing a man named Vince Mitchel. At Vince's insistence, the pair went camping, and to his amusement, Janis wore her glitzy silver boots. They fished, swam, went on long walks, and boated. Janis even cooked. She was happy to enjoy some more traditional fun. She liked the fact that Vince just wanted to spend time with her, but in the end she rejected his love, probably out of fear.

The biggest rock concert to date was to take place on a farm in Woodstock, New York, in August 1969. It was a triumphant event—hundreds of thousands of young people gathered peacefully for a festival of music and love. But in a sense, it was also tragic—thousands of kids were strung out on drugs, staggering, senseless, and listless.

Just before she went onstage, Janis and a friend shot up heroin in a portable toilet. Even after eight months of con-

time together. For the first time in a long time, Janis remained unclouded by drugs and was able to enjoy true intimacy with another person. The pair made a trip into the jungle. Other than the fact that Janis suffered a mild concussion after a motorcycle accident, the trip to Brazil was just about perfect.

Janis ended up spending five weeks in Brazil and kicking her heroin habit. The plan was for David and Janis to return to the United States together, but David was held up at the airport because of a problem with his passport. Janis flew home alone. Two days later, when Niehau arrived at Janis's door, he found a stranger. Janis was strung out on heroin, in a daze. She was not the woman Niehau had fallen in love with in Brazil.

A handbill for a Janis Joplin concert at the Fillmore West.

David saw that fame was killing Janis and tried to persuade her to quit show business. She refused but asked him to stay on as her road manager. He decided to leave and continue his trip around the world. Janis was, in a sense, all alone again. She had shut out everyone. Only her heroin was left to keep her company.

Seen here on the cover of her album *Pearl,* Janis's
record released in 1971.

ANOTHER PIECE OF MY HEART

In early 1970, Janis reinvented herself once again. After she and a friend talked about how essential it is for a performer to keep her personal self separate from her public self, she devised a new name for her stage persona—Pearl. Pearl was wild and raucous, clad in feathers and beads, hard-drinking, hard-living. Somehow, this alter ego made Janis feel better, more grounded.

Both Pearl and Janis continued to indulge in drugs. Janis could not stop—the pain was too real. When she was not doing heroin, she was drinking heavily. When a friend asked her if she felt better being clean from heroin, her answered revealed her desperation. "If you call drinking a quart of tequila a day being better, then I'm better."

The effect of the narcotics numbed the incredible pain Janis felt. It gave her a false sense of security, a rocky foundation on which she built her last days. She was undeniably addicted, but to her credit, she always seemed to resolve to stay clean no matter how many times she faltered.

She also had a new reason to keep off drugs. Janis formed a new band, the Full Tilt Boogie Band, in April 1970. Again, she saw a psychiatrist in an attempt to stay off smack, but she continued to drink.

Unlike her previous band, the Full Tilt Boogie Band played well together. They went on tour in May, and critics were impressed. "Howling, screeching and penetrating the air with . . . brilliance and force," exclaimed the *Louisville Courier-Journal*. David Dalton of *Rolling Stone* raved about Janis's spontaneity and professionalism. Finally, Janis had a band that could keep up with her. But life on the road brought out the worst in Janis. Stepping in front of crowds each night only exacerbated her loneliness and depression.

Friends tried to help alleviate some of the stress. As always, Janis was generous with her friends. She threw parties and as always would do just about anything for them, including providing them with drugs and alcohol. Part of this generosity was rooted in insecurity; she was afraid that if she did not give, people would not like her. On the other hand, she realized some people were using her to get drugs and money. She could not find the strength to strike a happy balance between these two extremes. In the midst of her depression and anxiety, she started making a lot of calls home to Port Arthur. She felt disconnected to everything and everyone, but at least she felt connected to her parents, despite the fact that she had spent so much energy trying to escape them.

In July 1970, Janis and the band started recording an album, called *Pearl*. The recording sessions were stressful, but they went well. She and her band members stayed in Los Angeles at the Landmark Hotel, where many rock singers stayed. They jokingly called it the Landmine.

During this time, Janis vowed not to socialize with friends who were also addicted to drugs. She managed to stay clean for a few weeks at a time, but her life had become a roller coaster of addiction. Janis started throwing even more temper tantrums. She was tired and lonely. She fantasized about quitting show business, getting married, and having a family, but she felt that rock and roll was all she had. She knew, in reality, that she was not made for the status quo life.

Nick Gravenites, Linda's husband, was angry at his friend's self-destruction. He told Janis that she concentrated too much on the larger, less tangible issues when, in fact, it was the small, more real things in life—friends, eating, cleaning the house—that mattered.

"I don't want to live that way," Janis spat back. "I want to burn. I want to smolder."

Bessie Smith had tremendously influenced Janis, both in her music and her personality. Janis related to the way Bessie lived: she drank hard, was unlucky at love, and sang the blues. The fact that Bessie Smith died an early death did not seem to affect Janis.

Janis overcame her depression long enough to visit her parents in Port Arthur. She garnered a lot of local media attention. On one hand, she craved it; on the other, she feared it. Not knowing how to deal with her mixed emotions, she behaved badly, probably out of insecurity. She gave a variety of sarcastic answers in most of the media interviews she took part in during that visit.

When she returned to California, Janis began dating Seth Morgan, a Berkeley student. Within a few days they were talking about marriage. He had his own money, which made Janis feel more secure about his intentions. She liked the fact that he loved her for herself and not her money. Soon, they started drinking heavily together.

Most of Janis's performances were marred by her state of drunkenness. Friends continued to voice concerns over her health and safety and tried to figure out how to get her into a halfway house to be treated for addiction. Janis had already overdosed several times from heroin. She knew of people who died of overdoses, but she still continued to use.

On September 19, 1970, Jimi Hendrix died of an overdose. The Associated Press asked Janis to comment. "I wonder what they'll say about me after I die," she said to a friend.

She and Seth had a fight—based on her insecurities about being used for her money. They were in a clothing store when Seth jokingly fingered a shirt, suggesting that Janis should buy it for him. Janis flew into a rage and accused Seth of using her.

Back at the hotel, she sobbed hysterically, afraid that he would leave her. But they made up, and life went along as usual. Janis was once again determined to improve her looks, probably in an attempt to impress Seth. Once again, she dieted and lost weight. She went to a beauty salon and had her hair streaked. She sat at the pool and got a tan. Since Janis did not usually spend much time fussing with her

WOODSTOCK

Janis Joplin

Janis was featured on the first-day issue of the
stamp commemorating Woodstock in the series
"Celebrate the Century: 1960s."

appearance, friends were impressed by her efforts. She looked good and healthy.

Later that week, Janis changed her will. A will she had drawn up two years earlier said that her entire estate should go to her brother, but she wanted to make sure that her parents and her sister were also included.

On Saturday, October 3, Janis made a few calls. She inquired about a marriage license at City Hall. She called a tailor about some new clothes. Later that afternoon, someone delivered a fresh supply of heroin to Janis's room. She shot up and then went to rehearsal.

Janis did not sing, but instead listened with a critical ear to the musical tracks. She was looking forward to recording the vocals the next day. On the way home, she, band member Ken Pearson, and another man stopped for a few drinks at Barney's Beanery. At about 12:30 A.M., Janis returned to her room at the Landmark Hotel. As usual, she had arranged her things—candles, lace, her favorite pictures, an Indian bedspread—around the room to make it more comfortable. Then she shot up.

She stopped in the lobby to get change for a five dollar bill so she could buy some cigarettes. When she got back to her room, she suddenly fell forward, still holding some change she had just received. Janis died of an overdose on October 4, 1970, at 1:40 A.M., at age 27.

Janis spent so much of her life escaping—from city to city, from friend to friend, from drug to drug. But what she probably did not realize was that, all along, she was trying to escape from herself.

Further Reading

Amburn, Ellis. *Pearl: The Obsessions and Passions of Janis Joplin.* New York: Warner Books, 1992.

Busnar, Gene. *Super Stars of Rock: Their Lives and Their Music.* New York: Simon and Schuster, 1980.

Echols, Alice. *Scars of Sweet Paradise: The Life and Times of Janis Joplin.* New York: Metropolitan Books, 1999.

Freidman, Myra. *Buried Alive: The Biography of Janis Joplin.* New York: Harmony, 1992.

Ward, Ed, Geoffrey Stokes, and Ken Tucker. *Rock of Ages: The Rolling Stone History of Rock and Roll.* New York: Rolling Stone Press, 1986.

Chronology

1943	Janis Joplin is born on January 19.
1949	Begins taking piano lessons.
1960	Graduates from Thomas Jefferson High School in Port Arthur, Texas; enters Lamar College but drops out after a semester.
1961	Earns her secretarial certificate at Port Arthur College; moves to Los Angeles.
1962	Returns to Texas and enrolls at the University of Texas at Austin; begins performing.
1963	Hitchhikes with Chet Helms to San Francisco; gets a singing gig in a coffeehouse her first night there.
1964	Travels to New York City, where she sings in clubs in the East Village; returns to California.
1965	Gets hooked on amphetamines; tries to check herself into a mental hospital; returns to Texas and reenrolls at Lamar.
1966	Returns to San Francisco and joins Big Brother and the Holding Company.
1967	Enjoys wild success at the Monterey Pop Festival; gets rave reviews.
1968	Begins drinking heavily; *Cheap Thrills* is released; Big Brother breaks up.
1969	Goes solo; forms her own band and goes on tour; they record *Kozmic Blues;* performs at Woodstock; plunges deeper into drugs; tries repeatedly to break her addiction but fails.
1970	Forms the Full Tilt Boogie Band; records *Pearl;* continues to abuse heroin; Janis dies of a heroin overdose in Los Angeles on October 4.

Discography

Albums

1968   *Cheap Thrills*

1969   *I Got Dem Ol' Kozmic Blues Again Mama* (Columbia)

1971   *Pearl* (Columbia)

1972   *In Concert* [live] (Columbia)

1975   *Janis Joplin* [OST] (Columbia)

1978   *Janis Joplin* (Supraphon)

1983   *Prime Cut* (Swinghouse)

       Farewell Song (Columbia)

1999   *Live at Woodstock: August 19, 1969* (Columbia)

       Full Tilt Boogie (Columbia)

Compilations

1973   *Janis Joplin's Greatest Hits* (Columbia)

1978   *Pearl/Cheap Thrills* (Columbia)

1980   *Anthology* (Columbia)

1993   *Janis* (Columbia/Legacy)

1995   *Cheap Thrills/I Got Dem Ol' Kozmic Blues Again Mama* (Sony)

       18 Essential Songs (Legacy/Columbia)

1999   *Ultimate Collection* (Sony International)

       Box of Pearls: The Janis Joplin Collection (Sony)

INDEX